I0172359

ISBN 978-0-9903713-0-4

9 780990 371304

50899

LaNisha Rene

A Girl's Journey
Setups to Setbacks on the Road to Success
The Limitless Ability to Achieve

A Girl's Journey Inc.

LR Consulting Enterprise, LLC

Published by:
A Girl's Journey, Inc.
a division of
LR Consulting Enterprise, LLC
Atlanta, Georgia

For more information:
E-mail to AGirlsJourney@LRConsultingENT.com, Reference Permissions subject line.

ISBN: 978-0-9903713-0-4

Manufactured in the United States of America.

Photo Credits: Ty Spencer

LaNisha Rene

A Girl's Journey Inc.

Dedication

This book is dedicated to all the girls who are just like who I use to be. I learned the hard way to succeed. I took chances, not all positive, to obtain what was rightfully mine, I refuse to allow you to go down the road I did. You have the right to a journey filled with unlimited opportunities.

I thank God who knew my journey before I did and for allowing me to go down the bumpy road of life, I've actually learned a lot about myself.

Thank you mother, Michelle Robinson, for giving what you could with what you knew how to give. I'm proud of your accomplishments and proud of you for changing your journey.

To my aunts, Christine Dixon and Sonya Dixon who never gave up on me, my grandmother, Joann Dixon, who raised all her grandchildren; providing us with what we needed, my departed grandfather, George Dixon, who influenced my entrepreneurial spirit, your baby girl did it pop-pop, and to my dad, Jerry Townsend, who left me. You helped me learn the hardest lesson in life, TO FORGIVE!

Thanks to all of my mentors who knew it was time for me to write this book and begin A Girl's Journey project. Marc Parham, who always saw my value; thank you for showing me how to meditate and relax! Thank you to my spiritual mentor, Bill Thompson, for all of your wisdom and love. Jenifer Duncombe, you helped me at a time I was at my weakest, thank you for your friendship, love, and dedication towards my recovery.

To my niece, Kahneya Teague, I grew up because of you. I didn't want you to be like me but better. You have so many great options in life no matter what road you started on; you can always change your direction but it will take hard work and dedication. Thank you for volunteering at events and participating in Phase 1 of A Girl's Journey. I will always make you proud of me!

Thank you to everyone who is reading this book and to those who have followed my career. I am grateful for your support and encouragement. May God touch your life and those around you!

"By wisdom a house is built, and through understanding it is established; through knowledge, its rooms are filled with rare and beautiful treasures."

A Girl's Journey Inc.

About the Author

LaNisha Rene Townsend is a published business columnist & creator of A Girl's Journey; a three phase mentorship development project working to build young girl's self-esteem. She holds a Masters in Business, Bachelors in Management & Bachelors in Psychology with 10+ years exp in business development, marketing, branding, communications, project management & public relations.

She's worked with multiple celebrities, developed varies businesses, written numerous business advice columns, hosted/co-hosted radio shows & was appointed Executive Editor for two girl-based publications (Kontrol Girl Magazine & Polish Magazine).

Throughout her journey, LaNisha has developed processes to help businesses run efficiently & consulted with major corporations like Wise Foods Inc., Advantage Sales & Marketing, At&t, The Partec Group, Atlanta Urban League, ABC Publicity, Partnership for Community Action to name a few.

During her time as Executive Editor/Contributor for Kontrol Girl Magazine, LaNisha began to listen closely to the girls; paying attention to their ideas, frustrations & thoughts in general. At the end of 2013, LaNisha chose to resign as Executive Editor. When she developed the mission for the magazine, she noticed it was not following the direction intended.

"Our goal was to build a socially conscious learning environment where girls benefited from the media; the stories & community activities should have been used to encourage the girls. It was our responsibility to foster a place of mentorship & unity."

In 2014, she became Executive Editor/Publicist for Polish Magazine but for several years, LaNisha has volunteered her time working with not-for-profit organizations giving business advice & speaking to the youth about staying in school; focusing on good vs. bad decisions & peer relationships. Her purpose is to motivate girls to be strong; an independent thinker continuously seeking positive people who can help them become successful on their journey.

A Girl's Journey Inc.

Lanisha Rene

Introduction

A Girl's Journey
Phase 1
Ages 13-16

Setups to Setbacks on the Road to Success
The Limitless Ability to Achieve
Taking PRIDE in Your Direction

"The lives we are given may not be our choice, but once we recognize & understand the difference between right from wrong, positive & negative; only then can we begin our journey."

Young girls aren't taken serious until faced with the consequences of their actions. But why do their actions lead to poor decision-making?

o   Parents' involvement and accountability?
o   Commonalities and generational curses?
o   Self doubt?
o   Ability to make smarter, responsibly decisions?
o   Follows the crowd?
o   No direction?
o   Lack of influence on their level of understanding?
o   Neglected and unnoticed by family and peers?

All of the above are common factors as to how and why many young girls fall victim to poor decision-making. Young girls want to be encouraged, yearn for positive reinforcement as well as genuine love from those who truly believe in their worth. In addition, these girls are lacking encouragement; resorting to receiving attention anyway possible to validate their self-worth even if it's a false representation of themselves. During the adolescence age, girls tend to view each other and of self more negatively which influences their academics, behaviors, and social skills.

As years of negative habits set-in or go unnoticed, the harder it becomes to break so a young girl's self-worth and esteem can be rebuilt. It's time to confront the brutal facts about why young girls fail before their given a chance.

Phase 1, helps girls ages 13-16 to understand the purpose of their future and how bad decisions can affect their success. Through building and/or re-building a path of limitless possibilities and changing the perspective on outcomes, A Girl's Journey uses methods that are statistically proven to aid in positive youth development such as self/peer activities, writing exercises, self-esteem encouragement, and affirmation challenges.

Most girls feel insecure in their decisions not only because they're inexperienced and young, but due to the lack of mentors who can relate on their level of understanding. I learned at an early age that our minds and bodies have unbelievable abilities we don't know exist until our survival instincts kick in. The youth today need courage, confidence, faith, determination, and a sense of direction. Our young girls must first be empowered to believe in themselves in a stable environment that teaches varies independent self encouraging activities and given the tools to communicate their thoughts and needs when necessary.

Self-Esteem
The Power of Self Satisfaction
Raising Your Self-Esteem

A Girl's Journey, Phase 1, is designed to help young girls change their attitudes, outlook, perception, and direction by first building a stronger foundation with the help of parents and peers. Parents are the guides while commonly, peers, and societal norms become the influencers.

As a young girl, someone I thought loved me, verbally and sexually abused me. Abandoned by my father and left to survive with no instructions from my mother, I was destined to FAIL! Growing up as a young girl, violence and abuse was all around me and was my perception of life.

I was walking through life backwards, looking for others to give me purpose (*not help me build it*) and give me self-esteem (*not help me achieve it on my own*); falling more into a revolving trap of needing others to define what I wanted or what I needed in life (*not help me seek it on my own*).

Here is where I went wrong; no one can give you purpose or self-esteem, notice the *"SELF"* in self-esteem. This type of *"POWER"* comes from within. Self-esteem helps one's confidence, builds worth and motivates self-respect.

This project teaches girls several confidence building activities, which includes positive interaction with their peers. Interactions and communicating positively with other young girls makes a difference in how positive self-esteem grows; encouraging others who may need positive motivation is a great purpose-filled path on the road to building greater self-esteem because of its benefits for both parties involved.

LaNisha Rene

"You have never really lived until you have done something for someone who can never repay you."

John Bunyan (English Christian writer/preacher)

Positive reinforcement that builds self-esteem individually and in others is crucial at this age. Low self-esteem is a negative thought of self and abilities; affecting emotions and reactions. This can be confusing for young girls; causing self-defeat and self-destruction. These actions tend to be automatic, impulse-driven, and can also be caused by early maturation.

"The creation communicates volumes about the creator."

Girl Facts:
Self-Esteem

Negative Self-Esteem   vs.   Positive Self-Esteem

Negative Self-Esteem	Positive Self-Esteem
Thinks critically about the world!	Grow up feeling secure!
Anger problems!	Take action, make positive choices, and do positive things for others!
Do not interact and choose not be involved in activities with peers!	Express feelings and acknowledge the feelings and thoughts of others in caring ways!

PBS Parents, Understanding and Raising Girls *"Raising a Powerful G*

Girl Facts:
Self-Esteem
Early Maturation

- Increases hormone production in adolescence and can produce dramatic growth spurts.
- Tend to experience more difficulty fitting in.
- May get teased because they are ahead physically and academically.
- May be less popular.
- Depression and anxiety are likely if not encouraged or motivated consistently.
- Tend to make friends with older peer groups.
- Exhibit body image problems and more conflicts with parents.

A girl who matures early doesn't necessarily mean there is anything wrong with her, it actually means the opposite. Maturing early simply means she develops and learns faster. However, this is something she must be careful with because it may cause the need to want to be a part of older crowds, which is not a bad thing, just make sure these crowds are a positive group of people your parents have met. A young girl can definitely learn from others who have experienced what you may be currently going through. Make sure to ask questions and learn from those older, positive crowds.

High self-esteem for girls who mature faster is crucial, as you can see from the bullets; they may have more problems socially, physically, and mentally. Although, there is nothing wrong with maturing faster, we have to be honest and know that when young girls differ from other young girls, especially in size, they are subject to teasing and many times, out casted by their peers. Girls who mature faster are just simply unique and there's nothing wrong or bad about that!

I matured must faster than a lot of the girls in middle school and high school but I also got into the wrong crowds with people who did not influence me, they actually didn't help me at all. I only become too fast for my own good, got into lots of trouble, and had a lot of bad habits. Unfortunately, all that knowledge I learned from the older crowds, I used in all the wrong ways.

Purpose
A Work in Progress

As young girls get older, matures, and gains more positive influence, their purpose evolves before they know its happening. Purpose takes patience combined with continual learning and growth; many can influence this but no one can give it to you.

The activities in A Girl's Journey project motivates positive thoughts and emotions with varies skill building and goal setting activities; influencing creative thoughts followed by actions. When one has purpose, they feel stronger, confident, and more certain in their decisions.

"Purpose gives the passion to achieve more."

In life, we have to decide what is important to us and what we would most like to see change in our life. Every girl wants to be a success. No girl sets out to fail but the truth of the matter is that many will. A huge challenge for young girls today is a sense of identity.

Girls are searching for a sense of purpose more than ever in these times of poverty, social and culture influencers, new era technology, and lack of parent involvement. Purpose makes us feel connected, valued, and significant. Without proper guidance, self-esteem, self-exploration, effective communication, cultural exposure, accountability, and support; it's difficult to maintain hope, causing a disconnect from family and friends, leading to bad decisions that introduce young girls to the juvenile justice system; which statistics confirms.

It is time for a new approach! A Girl's Journey takes a more intimate approach and reflects on an understanding of the realities of young girls today; the girls feel comfortable; not judged or discouraged to share their problems and emotions. They communicate with their peers in a positive and productive way that builds motivation and sense of security in others.

Phase 1 provides a transformative space for girls to create and participate in structures they can apply in their everyday life while learning the value of purpose and respect with fun-filled, self reflective activities.

Girl Facts:
Purpose Goes a Long Way

"One of the groups of adolescents at greatest risk of failing to make successful transitions to adulthood are delinquent youth who end up in the "deep end" of the juvenile justice system, in its detention centers and other locked institutions."

– The Annie E. Casey Foundation

According to Crime in the United States, 2011 (released in November 2012), during 2011: Nationwide, law enforcement made an estimated 12,408,899 arrests (does not include citations for traffic violations).

25.9% of arrests were of females.	13.7% of these arrests were under age 18.

Pay close attention to what is happening in this age group! Many young girls are failing due to confidence issues, low self-esteem, no direction, or purpose with a variety of other issues.

What A Girl's Journey wants young girls to take from this project is that we all have dilemmas and self-esteem issues; but it's how we give them power over our journey. When one knows their worth and direction, no matter what comes our way, with positivity, courage, and patience; life's issues will not hinder the road to success.

"We don't have to stay in the prisons of our past and bad habits."

Writing
The Power of Writing

Age 16 was the most disconnected and loneliest, as a teenager, I felt. I was scared, depressed and had given up on myself because I thought everyone else gave up on me. After dropping out of high school in the 9th grade, I can remember, sitting, staring into space.

"At our weakest, our heart and spirit continue to stay strong and subconsciously push us when our body and mind give up."

I noticed a sheet of paper and began to write. I wrote everything I thought about. I wrote to myself, I wrote about myself, I wrote what I expected from myself, I wrote about others, I wrote to others which also included poems. I wrote on sticky notes and in journals.

The most rejuvenating piece of work I wrote was a letter to me; expressing when I was last happy, how I felt about me and who specifically made me feel this way.

I am sharing these parts of my life to show girls I understand how they feel. It is time to release that anger and frustration.

Young girls need to learn that they will encounter people who will not always listen to their thoughts or issues but they cannot keep it bottled up; release those thoughts, release that anger, and release those feelings about everything happening through honest writing activities.

As the years passed, I continued to write more and more. As an adult, working on the activities for A Girl's Journey, I took a few friends aside and asked each to use four color markers, a poster board, and write different categories of what they feel associating each feeling with a color.

I call this activity the *"Journey Board"*. I learned a lot about my friends through this exercise and how to nurture our friendship and how to be a better friend. The activity also released feelings about themselves they never knew existed. Young girls will learn more about this activity in their workbook so use it wisely and open your thoughts to the experience.

"Draw a line between your past and future. Your past should not dictate your future."

Read the three letters below my niece (Kahneya) wrote to herself, mother, and grandmother. She has a lot of built up anger stored. Once she finished writing, she felt better and was no longer angry; she just needed to release her feelings of pain and anger.

"Sometimes, it's more productive to write down your words of frustration instead of speaking them because those words may not result in a positive conversation or outcome."

"*Dear Kahneya*,

I am sad because I want my mom, I am mad because I want to live with her. I don't mean to hurt other people, I just want my mom and when people start yelling at me, I just get scared then I get mad and things I don't mean come out and after I say all those hurtful words, I realize what I did and said wasn't right and I just really don't mean it. I ask for forgiveness but I know I might not get it because of how hurtful I was."

"*Dear Mom*,

I miss you, I would like to live with you, but you need to get your stuff together. If you get yourself together then what people say about you, I wouldn't care."

"*Dear NanNa*,

You know I love you but my mom is always on my mind and the questions I have about her. You yelling at me scares me then makes me mad. I am sorry for the things I said and what I said I didn't mean NanNa but can you calm down with the yelling at me because it scares me and brings out the little girl in me."

Kahneya Teague, Age 13

"The spirit of grief will hinder your life and inevitably hurt others."

Process of Writing
The Growth Process

Every action begins with a thought. Our imagination can bring about several opportunities if we just expand on them. With a little help from others, one's thoughts can produce some creative, interesting, powerful actions. When you write what you think, it becomes a reflection; turning thoughts into reality.

Writing helps to create plans and goals, releases anger, and builds on ideas, but most importantly, it shows growth; writing allows one to truly see all aspects of their life.

Before asking people I love to participate in many of my writing assignments, I was my first student. The Journey Board, showed me maturity, one of my sections were of negative words that came to mind when I thought of myself. I was happy and excited with my words, although the words were written out with a black marker and were negative thoughts I felt about myself; I still learned that most of the words I used to describe myself negatively last year were not the same words I use to describe myself today. The words I use today are more positive, happy, and joyful. I showed myself that I was growing, getting better at loving me, and recognizing my greatness.

It is always encouraging to go back and read your thoughts. Not only to reflect, but to also show progress on how these thoughts change and grow.

It can also be very healthy to read action words or action plans aloud. When you really listen and speak with confidence, knowing it will happen; it gives a sense of accountability, courage, and power; known as the law of attraction; attracting what you feel, think, and speak with positive energy for a positive outcome.

"Seek and you will find."

Matthew 7:7-8

"As our experiences change, we revise our expectations."

Girl Facts:
Process of Writing
Get an Action Plan

Consciously Think	Actions start with a thought.		
Write	See your thoughts.	Honest and Positive thoughts.	Create actions, goals, plans.
Speak	Speak aloud.	Be confident.	Be sure.
Do	What do you want?	How do you want to feel?	Who will you need to help you?

Confidence
Who You Are and Who You Are Not

We need people who recognize and influence our greatness. I realized, for me, it was my aunt Chris. One day, having a breakdown moment, feeling at my lowest; I called her crying, frustrated with life. I felt with so many things I was doing right, I couldn't understand why so much was going wrong. She first showed a sense of compassion with an apologetic spirit, followed by, "*Nisha, you come from a line of strong women; you are strong. But you need to occupy your time with things you like doing and that encourage you!*"

My aunt was right. She understood that although I was trying to be a better person and make smarter choices to improve myself; there will be situations and uncontrollable circumstances throughout life but I needed to find how and what would help control my reactions in a positive, encouraging way.

The conversation with my aunt put a lot into perspective for me; helping to bring my confidence back up. She reminded me of who I am and who I am not. She also reminded me of what I must do to remain who I am.

Without confidence, you cannot enjoy life. People who lack confidence are constantly frustrated, they feel cheated and robbed of their destiny, often feeling controlled or manipulated by other people because they quickly become people pleasers; spending most of their time pleasing everyone else except them self.

"We weren't created to live in fear or in a life of insecurities."

Not having confidence in yourself causes you not to stand up for your beliefs and notice when others are using you for their own selfish gain. If you have no confidence, fear of achieving will rule your future.

Girl Facts:
Top 5 Signs of Insecurity

1. Body Language
The way a person holds themselves can tell you if they are strong, confident and proud to stand tall and straight, or if they're trying to hide, shrink away, and just give up. The more open the body language, the more secure a person is likely to be, while closed body language (slumping, hunched shoulders, folded arms, etc.) suggests an insecure personality.

2. Controlling (bullying)
Sometimes people are so insecure about themselves that they have to lash out and pick on others in order to make themselves feel better.

3. Arrogance
Overcompensate for lack of confidence to elevate self.

4. **Compliments**

Not acceptant of a compliment or wanting to give one.

People who are insecure compare and compete all the time. They're constantly looking at someone else as a measure of what they should be and if they can't feel their better than, greater than, more than, their never happy with just being who they are.

Insecure people never grow up simply because they cannot handle any type of correction.

"No one can be truly confident until they face their weaknesses."

It's also healthy to recognize our weaknesses so we can make a conscious effort daily to either correct them or to determine when those weaknesses are hindering our positive progress.

Confident Attitude
Quality over Quantity

There is a saying in the field of marketing across the board, *"quality over quantity."* This saying is one I use professionally as well as personally because the saying can be used when we talk about a confident attitude as well. Although quantity is important, without the quality of a positive, confident attitude, quantity has no relevance. The quality of attitude is beneficial as well as important in our lives.

Quality is a feature many notice; a high level of value or excellence. Attitude is a way of thinking about someone or something; a feeling or thought that affects behavior.

To be confident and successful, your attitude has to be of good quality. The type of energy we put out towards others is the same type of energy we'll receive back in return; it's the Law of Attraction.

How we think about our self affects our actions and attitude but in order to not allow our actions to define our attitude, we must focus on positive thoughts and positive descriptive words throughout the day or whenever we feel doubt, anger or worry.

"If we are not impressed by our strengths, talents, and God given abilities then we can't be depressed by our weaknesses and inabilities."

Joyce Meyers

Attitude
Words
Actions

Positivity
Strength
Passion

Thoughts
Growth
Patience

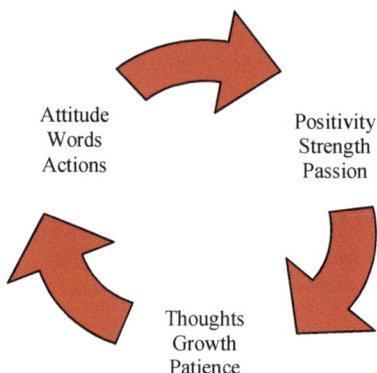

Most girls do not fear failure, it is the fear of not understanding when the decisions they make are the right choices.

To be successful, we must change our attitude, approach, and outlook on life; removing any and all negative factors in order to add positive influences that can help us on our journey. Being success requires hard work and dedication; learning from our mistakes so we do not repeat the same mistakes continually, and be around people who recognize our greatness who can pick us up when we fall.

I want our girls to have a fighting chance to succeed; a good start that leads them down the best roads possible on their journey with a positive sense of self because how we feel about our self impacts our journey and our relationships along the way.

So slow down young ladies and focus on quality over quantity! We can't expect our girls to be successful if we haven't given them the proper starting point! But, we also can't accept failure as an option either."

"Listen to advice and accept instruction, and in the end you will be wise."

Proverbs 19:20

A Girl's Journey Inc.

LaNisha Rene

Reference List

- National Criminal Justice Reference Service (NCJRS). Office of Justice Programs (2012). *Women and Girls in the Justice System* https://www.ncjrs.gov/spotlight/wgcjs/facts.html

- PBS. *Understanding and Raising Girls. Raising a Powerful Girl* (2014) http://www.pbs.org/parents/raisinggirls/powerful

- John Bunyan (2014) *His Life, Times and Work.* Wikipedia, the free encyclopedia http://en.wikipedia.org/wiki/John_Bunyan

- Zondervan Publishing House. The Spiritual Formation Bible (2014). *Growing in Intimacy with God through Scriptures.* New International Version. Grand Rapids. MI.

A Girl's Journey Inc.

Notes:
_____

_____

_____

_____

_____

_____

_____

_____

_____

_____

_____

_____

_____

_____

_____

_____

_____

_____

A Girl's Journey Inc.

Notes:_____

_____

_____

_____

_____

_____

_____

_____

_____

_____

_____

_____

_____

_____

_____

_____

_____

_____

_____

_____

LaNisha Rene

A Girl's Journey
Setups to Setbacks on the Road to Success
The Limitless Ability to Achieve

A Girl's Journey Inc.

LaNisha Rene

ISBN 978-0-9903713-0-4

9 780990 371304

5 0 8 9 9

www.ingramcontent.com/pod-product-compliance
Lightning Source LLC
Chambersburg PA
CBHW041809040426

42449CB00001B/31